MW01602876

The names, locations, and other identifiable information in these stories have been changed to protect the privacy of the story tellers.

Asperger Experts LLC
help@aspergerexperts.com
www.AspergerExperts.com

Special discounts are available on quantity purchases by corporations, associations, and others.

For details, contact us at: help@aspergerexperts.com

Struggling To Connect: Fatherhood With My Asperger's Child/Asperger Experts. —1st ed.
ISBN 978-1-945611-06-3

Contents

Introduction

In our work here at Asperger Experts, we hear from moms every day. They write in and tell us their concerns, ask for advice, and connect with each other on our website. They form support groups and get coffee together. They commiserate and share their experiences.

No such support is offered for dads. When we talk to fathers, they are often feeling confused, frustrated, and discouraged.

I remember when I was growing up, after being diagnosed with Asperger's at age twelve, my father and I struggled to connect for a while. But once we found common interests, we formed a strong bond that lasts to this day. But this book isn't about me.

Here at Asperger Experts, we believe in learning directly from those who have experienced it, because, as I'm sure you are well aware by now, there is a big difference between lived knowledge and book knowledge when it comes to Asperger's and Autism.

So we're bringing the experiences, mistakes, lessons, and stories of fellow fathers who have kids on the spectrum to you, so you can hopefully gain some new insight, a deeper perspective and some hope that things will turn out all right.

— Danny Raede & The AE Team

..•••••..

Developing a Different Relationship

I'm Marshall. I am the father of Jackson. He is sixteen years old. We knew something was different at around age two. We went through a bit of a process. I think he was three or four when he met with a psychologist, and he was four or five when he was officially diagnosed.

We had some ideas as we started meeting with the psychologist, and that psychologist was the first thing that really helped. We had great resources and day care workers, day care owners, and preschool teachers that helped us a lot with recognizing some of the differences with our son that led to diagnosis, but it was the actual diagnosis itself that helped us know how to help him better. It helped us understand what made him tick and understand why he couldn't relate to us in the way that we wanted him to.

When Jackson was little, as we were figuring things out, noises would set him off. He was a loner and wouldn't interact with other kids and other people. With my other kids, they'd run up and give hugs and spend time with family and friends. When they cried, they'd come to my wife and me. But Jackson wasn't like that. When he cried, he would push away and run away. My wife was his person and still is his person, and every now and then he'll come up and give her squeezes.

It was hard for me because he wouldn't relate to me on the level I wanted him to, and it felt like he didn't like me. I was just so used to kids that would show their affection. So he and I didn't have much of a relationship. During the times that I would want to be there for him as a dad, when I could tell he needed something, he wouldn't let me be there. When he was just a kid running around, he wanted to be by himself and do his own thing.

I'm a very loving person. I like hugs, and I'm pretty outgoing, so for me, it was really hard. It was really hard to think that this kid that I love with all my heart, might never have a relationship with me, or that I wouldn't be able to talk to him or help him when he had questions. He didn't understand what I was trying to do to help. He didn't see what I was trying to do as being helpful. It just broke my heart.

It wasn't until around the age of eight or maybe nine that he started to realize that I cared about him and that I was actually smart and knew a couple of things. He's highly intellectual and loves to have deep conversations, so when we left the area of needing purely emotional support to more of being able to have advanced conversations, we finally started to build our relationship.

He was also starting to become more self-aware and wanting to figure out what being on the spectrum meant, how it affected him, and how he could get along with the world. It's neat to see him learn and figure out emotion. I think he's learning from others how he should feel or should react. Whether he actually feels it or not, he's able to at least figure some of those social cues out where before he couldn't. From the intellectual conversations we started having, he recognized that I had some intelligence and that I had value and

2

worth beyond just being a person to provide for the family.

For Father's Day, we did a video for my church and asked the kids, "What is it that you love about your dad?" His comment was that he could turn to me and ask the hard questions, and I was always there for the conversation and those kinds of things.

The Difficulties We Still Have

There are still difficulties. When he was younger I know he was looking for safety and security, but sometimes I still question whether he recognizes the emotions of love, trust, and other feelings. I think he understands them from an intellectual perspective, but does he actually feel it in the same way I do?

About two or three months ago, he made a statement that he didn't really see a need for having a family, that he didn't see the need for having me and my wife. He didn't see a need to have a relationship, and to me that was another jab in the heart.

We figured out that what he was trying to communicate is that he gets strength from his friends and that he feels safe and comfortable with us, but yet, it just wasn't the same emotional connection. It was just his way of expressing the way he connects to the family. He knows family cares about him, but he gets more strength from his interactions with his friends and other things outside, instead of his relationship with his family, and I think it's because he knows that we're not going anywhere.

But to me, what I heard was, "I don't want to be a part of this family, and I'm not really interested in being a part of this family. I'm going to go do my own thing." That's hard, because to me, family is really important. But now he understands how we feel and why we misunderstood what he was trying to tell us.

He's still a teenager, so there are still times when he acts like a teenager. I have to think to myself, so are you acting like this because you're on the spectrum? Or are you acting like this because you're a teenager? Or is it both? But I think that it's been fun to see him grow because he is figuring out who he is. He's such a neat and amazing kid. The kid is so talented. He's so smart. That's the thing. We've always told him how brilliant he is

It's also nice because I think he's recognizing how our relationship as dad and son is different than that of a friend relationship. He's starting to come into an understanding of the differences between certain kinds of relationships.

For me, just knowing that we do finally have a relationship is amazing. There is a level of love and emotion in our relationship and he looks at me differently from some other guy that he would have a really great intellectual conversation with. He has great relationships with teachers, but I think he still recognizes our relationship as being a little bit different than that because we are father-son. So that's helpful to me. I really feel like he knows I'm his dad and that I care about him as a dad.

Advice for Other Dads

My advice to other dads would be to never give up. Know that even if they don't get it, love them like you would anyway. You're the dad. The dad doesn't ever go away. My wife and I both have worked really hard within and outside the school systems to figure out what his needs are, and I think that that's really the greatest thing—just recognizing each kid is different and figuring out what makes them tick and how to interact with them.

The fact I never gave up and kept working to care for him the best that we could from whatever distance he would let us helped maintain and grow that relationship too, because I didn't treat him differently. I still loved him and cared for him and told him I loved him. I still did all the other things I would do for my other kids as well, knowing

4

that sometimes he might not reciprocate it and might not show it back or might not understand what I was saying or doing. But I knew that I was doing all I could to care for him and to let him know that he had a family that loved him, cared for him, and was there for him.

You always want to do everything you possibly can even though they may not be able to communicate with you the way that you want them to. But know that if they're struggling to communicate with you, they're probably struggling to communicate with others. So we've always been our kids' biggest advocate and support, and I think that's the main thing. Advocate for them, support them, and show them love whatever way you can even if you don't feel that it's reciprocated. If you've got a kid on the spectrum, you've got a great kid, a neat kid, and learn to appreciate them for who they are. My kid fascinates me every single day, and I'm grateful that God gave me this opportunity to be a part of his life.

Chapter Two

..∙●●●●∙..

A Diagnosis that Changed My Life

My name is John and I was diagnosed with Asperger's when I was thirty-two. I got diagnosed because someone said to me, "You know your son's autistic, right?" They just casually assumed that we must know. So I started diving into everything I could read about autism and Asperger's. I never really paid any attention to it before, because my son always acted like me when I was his age.

The process of diagnosis for both my son and myself went relatively smoothly. I think we're pretty lucky in that regard. It still took a while though. We went to the normal doctor for my son, and then they recommended us to a pediatric specialist, where it took several months to get in, but once we got to see the specialist they confirmed the diagnosis of Asperger's for my son who was three at the time.

In the meantime, I also talked to my doctor, and then they took a long time looking around to find a psychologist that would be a good fit for what I was looking for. So I got lucky, because it seemed like they really spent a lot of time looking for a proper one. I've heard a lot of horror stories, but for me I had a great psychologist. I got diagnosed relatively quickly as well. Both my son and myself got diagnosed within a few months of being aware of Asperger's.

The diagnosis was the inciting incident to change a lot of beliefs I held. I held deeply onto a lot of fear and parented from that fear. When I first had my son, I thought, "I'm going to be a good parent. I'm going to do everything the right way!" That didn't work out well, and the diagnosis for both my son and me was the impetus that opened the door to realizing how different everyone's life experiences could be, thus allowing more acceptance and awareness into my own life.

It was a huge period of realizing that there were many things I was normalizing. It's amazing to see what you can dismiss if you don't have all of the information. All sorts of sensory sensitivities are things I dealt with. In the past, I would just assume that, for example, everyone just deals with awful clothing, not knowing that it was my sensitivity to the clothing that was the issue, not badly manufactured clothing, so I wouldn't say anything. There are a lot of random things like that, where I didn't realize how I would almost torture myself through normalization without realizing it. That opened up the door of realizing that I didn't need to torture myself through normalization anymore, and my son didn't either.

Through therapy, I became more accepting, more open minded, and more willing to question certain assumptions that I had held beforehand. Something I struggled with before was that at my core, I had a lot of opinions and beliefs, but I was too afraid to live that way and express them. Now it is a lot easier just to say, "This is what works for us," and not question what the "right" way is. That was a major shift that led to a lot of revelations like starting to question things and say, "This isn't normal," or "This isn't healthy," or realizing that just because it is normal doesn't mean it is healthy. So a lot of things quickly changed once I started down this path.

I think the reason why I was so willing and able to accept both my diagnosis and my son's diagnosis was because of how I grew up. For other dads, it definitely depends on their own experiences growing up, although if you grew up autistic or especially if you didn't know, you were very likely to experience many difficulties. Specifically, I found there was a big problem in my life with adults and this obsession with authority as a way of handling things. Every time that I didn't respond in a way someone expected, most likely I was going to be met with authority, whether that was in school, or with parents, or with whomever. In my childhood, I was either usually facing neglect or loss of control, not really anything in between.

The diagnosis was such a world-view change for me. It wasn't just information, it was a big deal for my own acceptance, and it opened this door of just realizing to what extent everyone's experiences can be different. That made it easier to start being accepting of not just myself, but of everything. The combination of the protectiveness I felt over our son, of not wanting him to ever feel really bad like I did growing up, plus getting us diagnosed at the same time was a really powerful combination. It made sense.

In essence, getting diagnosed allowed a world-view shift that caused me to have more and less tolerance. More tolerance in terms of ways people did things differently, and less tolerance of all the crap in the world that I dealt with as a child that I had previously normalized.

Before we were diagnosed, I basically had zero boundaries, because I was just trying to avoid problems all day. I was walking around on eggshells all the time, or sometimes I was just hoping that I didn't cause someone to get mad at me. I was just trying to constantly avoid that. That became overwhelming because I kept trying to tell myself, "Oh well, I just won't do that thing next time," which became more and more limiting.

I have to give a lot of credit to my therapist for helping me to start realizing that I was doing the best I could in most situations. My therapist taught me about being nicer to myself. Before, there was this feeling of "If I go easy on myself, I can't get better. So I have to be really hard on myself every time I mess up."

Now I tend to ask myself, "Did I do the best that I could in that situation realistically?" Most of the time the answer is "Yes, yes I did." Then you know what? I'll learn from this. But I'm not going to beat myself up. I did what I could.

That also applied, obviously, to our son. Before the diagnosis, my parenting approach was this "Super Nanny" style of authority and force and saying, "This isn't acceptable. So therefore, I'm going to force the correct way of doing things."

He's nine now, so it's been a pretty long time...almost five years. He still randomly brings up things from my "Super Nanny" years of wanting to control everything about him. He will come up to me and ask, "Do you remember when you did this to me? You made me stay in one spot and I was really upset." When he does that I just apologize. I don't really excuse it, I just apologize. I'm glad that we are in a place where we're comfortable enough to talk about these things now. Before it may have been easy to dismiss them and say, "Well, I'm doing what I have to do as a parent."

I think I was so mad inside about all the times people were clearly trampling over me, but I didn't feel like I could do anything because I was "being irrational" or "not keeping the peace" according to my parents. It gave me all the right tools at the right time. I think when you grow up with different experiences than the norm, you kind of get unintentionally gaslit a lot. Even things like saying, "This hurts," or "This is bothering me." Kids tend to get dismissed in general, but especially if it's an experience that people can't relate to. I used to hear "Oh, there's no way that can hurt," or "Stop being over-dramatic."

Often, when I was growing up, I saw people do things that didn't line up, so that made me doubt my own reality a bit. So having a therapist was a sanity check. I could say to myself, "OK, this person hasn't doesn't known me before this. There's no reason for them to lie to me." Even though there were people in my life who tried to reassure me, it was very easy to dismiss any compliments or positive feedback as, "Oh, they're just trying to be nice." It was very easy to be programmed to dismiss them, or assume that I must be wrong.

My therapist was the last piece that fell into place to really give me assurance that I wasn't being unreasonable with myself by setting expectations and holding boundaries. Much of the stuff in therapy should be stuff that everyone's just taught. It seems like a huge mistake that a lot of these things aren't taught to us as kids. One of the biggest shames to me is that a lot of people treat the idea of needing therapy as an insult. In my opinion, we all need some sort of help. It's difficult to navigate life alone and we, as humans, aren't designed for that.

The great thing about a good therapist is that it is very patient-focused. Oftentimes, you're the one driving the exploration, and the therapist is acting as a guide. Or, like I said earlier, for me it was a sanity check. For a lot of my therapy, I was driving the revelations and the therapist was just giving me a space where I could safely talk about my thoughts and have someone validate me. If you're by yourself and you're struggling, even if you have helpful thoughts that enable you to hold healthy boundaries and change your perspective, you probably won't trust them. You might doubt them, and then you'll start to default to your normal pattern, which generally isn't helpful.

My Son's School Experience So Far

Going back to the story of my son, overall, pre-k went pretty well because we had good communication with teachers. The other major factor was that we had the diagnosis shortly before he started and as a result we had the understanding, tools, and ways of communicating his needs going in. It probably could have gone much, much worse if we didn't have that information from the beginning. We did have a few problems whenever there were student teachers, and that was where I started to realize that some of the ways that the school normally did things just wasn't going to work for us. For instance, we prepped in advance a lot and gave the teacher tons of instruction. For example, laying out ways to help when our son was struggling and approaches for communicating with him more effectively, but we found that when there was a student teacher, they would often not pass on any of that information.

When I asked why, they said that because of privacy concerns a lot of parents actually preferred not to pass that info on. People get so worried about people knowing their kids' diagnoses because they don't want people to know there's something wrong. To me, I don't see anything that says a diagnosis means there is something wrong. It's just information to make it easier for everybody. Unfortunately, I think that mindset is baked in.

Pre-k ended, which he loved, and then when kindergarten started, he went for a few weeks and then started refusing to go to school. I think the reason for the sudden school refusal was a combination of things. At the time we were in New York. This might vary by state, but pre-k in New York is still relatively open-ended. He could dictate a little bit more what was happening and it was more fun. Kindergarten feels like it's when they start to ramp up, get serious, and do it with less fun and more structure. So I think that was one factor.

Another that we learned in time was that our son was also pretty bored in kindergarten. I remember sitting at kindergarten orientation and realizing that he was not going to do anything new that year. They weren't doing anything that he didn't already know, because he really enjoyed math at a young age, as well as reading, and was already ahead.

There might be situations where they're going over a book and maybe he jumps ahead or corrects the teacher, but then he gets called out for disrupting the class when he's actually just trying to be helpful. I can remember experiencing that myself in school. I wasn't thinking about it as correcting. I was thinking, "I'm helping by giving you a right answer here." That can lead to problems. If you correct a teacher, many of them will take offense to it. Like, you've somehow soiled their respectability by correcting them. And some parents react that way too. They see it as almost like a threat, like you've undermined their authority in front of other people.

Another thing that went on was that this was the year they started the behavior chart, which is one of my least favorite things that's super popular now. We told the teachers, "That's not to be used on him." But of course, he couldn't escape the fact that it's going on around him. You could tell they were trying to hype the idea of a behavior chart up for us. They would say things like, "I worry he might feel disappointed because other kids are getting stickers for this thing." Once you add that manipulation dynamic in an environment, and even if you opt-out, he was still surrounded by it, so it does play into things, unfortunately.

Homework in kindergarten was optional, but he got stickers for it. It's one of those things where, in reality it was "optional," but they really wanted him to do it. They were just going to try to make him choose what they thought was the right thing by offering him stickers or some other reward. Since our son wasn't participating in the behavior chart with the stickers and rewards, it was truly optional for him. Sometimes he wanted to do it because he enjoyed whatever the activity was. And sometimes, he just didn't care and so he didn't do it. And that was fine by us.

The fact is that he was really, really miserable in kindergarten. Basically, he was just expected to shut up, be quiet, and sit there. He wasn't engaged in any way. If you think about it from his perspective, his thought process was, "I can go to school and not talk to anyone, or I can stay home and at least be a part of my family." The part of school he still liked was socializing, and it's always funny because people make comments about homeschooling and lack of socialization. But from my perspective, and my son's experience just being in kindergarten, you don't go to school to socialize. You get in trouble for that.

We used to take turns sitting at his lunch, and I always found it really uncomfortable, because usually they got a very short period of time, and there were a couple of supervisors yelling at the kids to be quiet and eat faster all the time. Even the one time when they theoretically could talk to their friends, they were rushed along and never given time. It was surprising to see such a huge shift from someone who just absolutely loved school and was so excited about it, and then a few weeks into kindergarten was just completely done.

At home, he was doing a lot and learning stuff on his own. From his perspective, he was thinking, "If I can't talk to my friends and I can't learn anything, and I can't do anything, why would I want to just sit there for six hours?" We were moving across the country not too long after that, so it was one of those things where my wife and I agreed that we weren't going to make him go. After the move, we decided not to reenroll him because he was still learning on his own and doing well.

He's now nine, and he's just been home since kindergarten. In fact, if school gets mentioned now, he'll still adamantly respond negatively at the mention of school. So we're taking a very unschooled approach. Some of the ways we're able make this work is the fact that I'm the only one who needs to work, and I'm able to work from home. So we're both home, which is a huge help.

Also, he's pretty self-driven. He's getting old enough now where I am starting to think about making sure that we're engaging with other types of topics just to get some variety in. Before he even started school, I had already showed him some animation in Adobe Flash. Since then, he's done his own videos, using Adobe Premiere or Scratch. He's always doing creative stuff.

I think people have a hard time envisioning learning without structure in the traditional, "I'm going to sit in front of someone and learn" style of learning. I think that there is a place for that, but I think that the idea of that being the only way to learn is fundamentally flawed. Most people's experience of learning is where you sit down in a class and absorb information. Then when you actually use it, you're not able to remember anything. Usually, you remember it for a task, because you have it for something. Whereas, if I'm programming or doing something myself, and I don't know how to do a particular thing and I go look it up, then I'm probably going to remember that because I had the context of why I wanted to use it when I did it.

I really don't like how math is taught in school. I always loved math, but in school, you're taught math in kind of a very paint-by-numbers approach. For example, you're given an equation, but you're not usually given meaningful context of how you'd use the equation in the real world. In fact, usually, you get these really horrible, word problems that aren't really realistic scenarios. They're worded in a weird way to trick you or test you, versus giving you context as to why a certain learning concept is useful.

My Advice for Parents

Now that my son is older, there are days where I think we need to be doing more. There's always an internal battle of feeling like you're never doing enough and there's always going to be a feeling like there's more you can do. But at the same time, I'm regularly surprised by the things he's doing on his own. Like being really into Roblox or Scratch, or other online communities. He's actually built up a little following of friends and communities on these online spaces, and I'm constantly surprised at how he's able to handle and express himself. I can't imagine being able to express myself like that at nine years old. I'm constantly amazed at how naturally a lot of this stuff happens. I'm happy that he is socializing a bit online. While that's something that I would like more of in-person, the balance can be different for everyone.

I think sometimes, we forget how a lot of these things are learned through life. Many times, as the parents, you can get in the wrong mindset by trying to figure out how to get this person to do more. I've realized I don't always need to get him to do more. I could throw a random documentary on, and he's going to be really interested in that. It gives us something to talk about.

My advice to parents that are just starting out, have just gotten diagnosed, and have no idea where to turn is this: When I was in the "Super Nanny Mode," I always thought that I needed to parent a certain way. I thought that I had to make them do the right things. I think many of those things are well intentioned, but I would still go back to the same framework of presenting opportunities. They really need to be the ones driving things themselves. In a lot of cases it really changes them.

Certain therapies could be very helpful. The main factor in whether or not the therapy is going to be helpful or healthy for you is whether you want to be there. If the therapy is being forced upon you, you are not going to be taking away the lesson that's intended at all. There's a very good chance it's going to harm you. I think this is true for any therapy. It's easy to look up accounts of people who were harmed by something like cognitive behavioral therapy (CBT), which isn't inherently bad, but it can definitely be used in a way that can harm someone if they're not on board with it.

I see all these teenagers that are in their room, in Defense Mode, aren't willing to engage because of all the battles that have already occurred, and have already been to fifty therapists and don't want to have anything to do with more drugs or doctors. They want to sit in their room and play video games all day long. How did they get there in the first place? Most of the time, if they're at that point, it was forced upon them to "make everything better."

That can be a really long process, especially if there's been a lot of that done. Because that probably means that there was a lot of harm. Sometimes you need to rebuild your relationship with your child so they can trust you and not feel like they need help because you thought there was something wrong with them.

I remember when I was growing up at that age, most of what I heard from adults had good intentions, but I heard a lot of fear-mongering stuff too. I just remember this idea of me bringing up things and not being able to "get away with this crap in the real world."

All that really did was make me feel like I was on a forced march to a really bad place.

I felt like the message I was getting was, "So you're telling me this is going to get worse?" Of course then I'm going to want to do whatever I can to feel good now! That doesn't incentivize me to do things differently. If anything, that's going to make me want to buckle down more, because you're telling me that it's actually really good right now, even though I feel terrible. But it's just going to get worse.

I think it's tough as a parent, but I think really, the solution is just about finding ways to be engaged and spend more time with your kid and have a trusting relationship. Because really, as a parent, you don't want to be an authority figure. It doesn't mean that there aren't situations where you have to make them do something that they don't want, because those situations do arise. But in general, that should be always be the least amount possible. In my eyes, me being the authority should only come up in situations where there is an immediate danger or harm that I have to prevent.

It should be more of an actual relationship where there's mutual respect and trust built up, because that's what really allows me to then have those conversations to figure out what my kids really want, so that I can collaborate and figure out an approach. That's when they open up and feel like they can have ideas and try things without fear of failure. That way, if they mess up, it's not as big of a deal anymore, because they know that I'm supportive anyway.

Chapter Three

..•●●●•..

Nurture a Little Bit More

My name is Jeremy and I'm the father of a now eighteen-year-old Asperger's child. He was diagnosed when he was around three or four years old.

He has a twin sister, and they were both born three months premature. So they were in the NICU for three months and when they came home, they were on heart and lung monitors. They had a lot of therapists. As an infant, they had a couple of therapists that actually came up to us and said, "You might want to keep an eye on your son. He's kind of showing some tendencies of autism."

At about age three or four, it started getting to the point where I could discipline his sister, but I couldn't discipline him. There was just a disconnect. It just seemed to make things worse. And at that point, we got him tested, and then the diagnosis of Asperger's was confirmed.

I like to dig in and I'm an analytical guy, so once the therapist told us that this could be a possibility, that's actually when I started reading and started researching it a little bit. Initially, there was a little bit of disappointment. But on the other hand, and in doing the research, I found out that people with Asperger's are some very talented people. My son didn't fit in with what I originally hoped for in a son, but he's got a lot of value, talent, and love that I needed to nurture in a slightly different way.

So for example, I'm a big baseball nut. I played it. I love to watch it. But it's not for him. We can't take him to a ballgame, and that's something I just had to accept. But there are other things that he's interested in that I also actually find fascinating too, particularly related to science. He loves to read Stephen Hawking books and things of that nature. When you have kids, you want your kids to be able to relate to some of the same interests that you have, but even though it wasn't exactly what I had been hoping for, it was still awesome. It's kind of like a video game. Once I master it, I stop playing it. So as long as there's a challenge ahead of me, then I want to keep playing because it is really interesting.

Changing Methods

I knew there would be some rough things along the way. The real eye-opener was trying to discipline him. We're not talking about corporal punishment or anything like that, just time-outs. It seemed like the more I did it, the worse everything became.

My wife actually pulled me aside and said, "Hey, this isn't working. You need to nurture a little bit more." So I started observing my wife because she's a little bit better with nurturing my son. So I did what I did best, and went to go learn. Like I said, a lot of books. I think the first book I read was by Temple Grandin. That was a real eye-opener for me as to what was going on, and everything just changed from that point forward.

We still have some rough patches. He still has some sensory issues that we're trying to work through that affect everyday living. But by and large, we're just trying to deal with it the best we can.

Starting in school, he had an issue sitting still. He didn't have a lot of sensory issues at that point. Or at least if he did, he wasn't showing them. I suspect he probably did have sensory issues, and was just good at hiding it. We very quickly got an IEP and all that set up for him. So we had aides from the beginning.

We're kind of lucky to be in the school district that we are in. It's a public school district, but they have a lot of resources and they're intertwined with a lot of local organizations that are already starting to work with him on volunteering and trying different work-related tasks.

We have some help from the government and he's got a Medicaid waiver. We've got legal guardianship to help him make some decisions until he's ready to do that. So we're in the transition phase right now to try and figure out what he's going to do next. I'm not sure if he's going to go into education, or continue his education, or if he's just going to go to work. I would think it's probably going to be education related because he likes science and likes to do research and stuff like that.

Life at Home

At home it's really important to him to have his own space. So, he's got a couple of spaces, one in the basement and another in his bedroom. We give him this space here at home to let him decompress and do whatever he needs to do.

Sometimes he acts out. For example, he gets upset if anybody's chewing around him. There are some other behaviors that trigger him, like if someone is clearing their throat. Sometimes that will bother him. Snoring really bothers him too. If he gets triggered, what I've realized is best is to not try to punish him for it. Just recognize that he's in the moment, and then give him space to get out of it or help direct him to one of his hideaway spaces.

As far as spending time together, we'll talk about things like outer space. He likes black holes and stuff like that, and to be honest, I don't fully understand everything he tells me, but he seems to get it. Like I said, he likes to read Stephen Hawking books and talk about those sorts of things. So we try to connect on that.

As far as activities go, we try to get him out as much as we can to spaces where there's not a lot of people. Usually hiking is really good for him. Museums are good, but what we'll usually do is call ahead to the museum and ask them for times when things are pretty quiet. So that way, we can at least work around some of the sensory things. When you can't work around those things, it's all about patience and trying to direct him out of the situation the best we can or trying to explain to other people around him what's going on.

As a parent, a lot of my ability to stay sane and calm comes from experience. I come from a high-pressure job, so I've just programmed myself to think certain ways. There are some Asperger's tendencies that I have myself that I've kind of worked through, but I think the same way he does. When you get in those high-pressure situations, at least in my opinion, it doesn't do a lot of good to scream and whine about it. You just have to move to the next step. That's all I do.

So for example, if my son is reacting, I won't yell at him. That doesn't do any good. I just think to myself, "What's the next best thing I can do?" It's just constant. I'm a problem solver, and that's what I do for a living. I do a lot of IT support. I work with clients that buy our software that costs them millions of dollars, literally. So the pressure is always there. So just as I've gone through my career, when something comes up, you just move to the next step. Instead of thinking about how bad it is, my brain goes immediately into problem solving instead.

That's actually one of the things I'm trying to work through with him to varying degrees of success: getting him to think about solving the problems rather than ruminating. When he gets in the moment and has these reactions, on the one hand, the reaction is normal and it's going to happen, but on the other hand, I try to get him to think that, "OK, I'm going to react. I'm going to scream and yell, but I also have to get to the next step." So if I can get him to think that way, that'd be great, but if not we'll just find another way to work it

Advice for Other Dads

I would encourage other dads to look at the same things that I did. Just start researching. I'd recommend that Temple Grandin book, As I See It. Then from there, they can kind of branch off and research other things in more detail however they want. But that's the number one thing: They need to research it and get all the information they can.

I'd also tell other dads that you've got to be extremely patient, and you've got to learn when to back off. That's where it's really helpful for me to have my wife who's very good at that stuff, because she'll check me. I still have issues every now and then, where I screw up too. I'm not saying I've got this all nailed down, like every other parent on the planet I'll slip up sometimes.

Ultimately, it comes down to patience. And by patience, I mean not only in dealing with them when they're in the moment, but also as they get older and progress (or lack thereof). You realize that they're not going to launch like other kids are. They're not going to get to seventeen or eighteen like I was and be ready to get out and go. It may take them a while. Depending on where they are on the spectrum, a lot of kids or young adults don't leave until maybe in their late twenties or around thirty-ish. But you've got to be patient, each kid's different, let them find their way and they'll let you know when they are ready. Our son has already started to make steps in that direction. He knows that he has to do these things to become an adult, and so he's more willing to do them.

I think the main thing I always tell everybody is that these are tremendously talented people, more so than, say, myself or my wife. They have tremendous talent. Their focus on what they're interested in is just laser sharp. As a parent, it's not about you. It's about them. You've got to find out what works best for your child.

Don't expect to have this child grow up and be a superstar athlete or a fantastic speaker or whatever. They're going to choose their own road, and you just have to push them in that direction. So rather than deciding for them and pushing them, you need to let them choose, and then you get behind them and push them in the direction that they're already going in.

Chapter Four

...•●●●...

Not Worse Just Different

My name is Shane and I have one son who is thirteen who has high-functioning autism. He probably would have received the diagnosis of Asperger's, but they don't technically give that diagnosis anymore.

He was about eight years old when we got the diagnosis. I know for some dads, that's a big emotional ordeal in thinking that there's something different with their kid, and others don't care and are actually grateful. My wife, who's an elementary school teacher, had driven most of the diagnosis process, so she recognized a lot of the things long before I did and put him into occupational therapy prior to getting an actual diagnosis. To be honest, once we got the diagnosis, it confirmed what we had already been working toward, and it was more of a relief, so that we now knew what we were dealing with and we could work to help him get what he needs.

The doctor told us, because of the diagnosis, he was entitled to an IEP, and he even warned us that the school may resist us on an IEP and just put it at a 504. The main difference is the amount of resources that the school will dedicate. They don't want to be on the hook because it's more effort and more resources. We applied for an IEP, and the school argued against it and gave us a 504 plan. Either way, he got some accommodations, which definitely helped in elementary school.

Early on, in those third, fourth, and fifth grades in elementary school, the 504 plan worked fine. We would have a meeting, the teacher would tell us what his struggles were, and we would make suggestions about what works for us. We had two meetings a year, and it worked really well.

Generally, the teachers were able to adapt. For example, he gets through his work faster than most, so we suggested to the teacher that if he got his work done in class, then they should allow him to just read. That way he's not getting frustrated and he's content.

As he got to middle school, though, we noticed a bit of a difference in the teachers' expectations and the 504 plan. Elementary school teachers are much more hands on, much more willing to handhold to a certain extent. In middle school, it's a little bit more about teaching kids independence. We struggled early in sixth grade with organizational skills. He was just not set up well when given an assignment to budget time out and create a plan. He fell behind fairly quickly. We had to scramble with the teachers to get that back online.

When he's engaged in the subject matter and he likes his teacher, everything goes smoothly. If there's some disconnect, meaning he doesn't innately understand the subject matter and/or doesn't have a connection with the teacher, then he just shuts down. For example, we found out in our 504 meeting in the middle of seventh grade that he was sitting under his desk for most of math class and completely shutting down. Apparently that had been going on for a few weeks.

As we get closer to high school, we are pushing for an aide or some form of counseling service to meet with him one-on-one. The hope in high school is that he will have more chances to meet with people and check in on a regular basis. The high school that his sister goes to has a robust inclusion program, not just for autism, but for any type of disability.

Utilizing Resources

Thankfully, even long before middle school there have been some great resources that have been available to us since the diagnosis. There were several clinics at the doctor's office that we went to that were really helpful. They had things like a feeding clinic that we were able to get involved in, a pill-swallowing clinic so that we could get more supplements in him to help with the eating, and a blood-draw clinic so that we could help him with getting tests done.

The pill-swallowing clinic teaches children how to take a pill in a progressive way. They start off by swallowing sprinkles that you put on your ice cream, and then a slightly larger pill, and then work their way up. Some of the supplements that he takes, like magnesium and fish oil, come in fairly large pills, so it was a way to get him to be able to swallow those.

Because he was such a picky eater, the feeding clinic introduced him to new forms of food. And again, that was the same concept where an occupational therapist set up a plan for him to get him to try new foods in small increments at a time. Each week we would have him pick out and try a new food. It helped to expand the amount of food that he was able to consume, and then we were able to dial back on some of the supplements.

We expected some resistance to these new processes, but once we explained the reason why, he was generally okay with it. The idea of breaking up his routine to go where we want him to go all of the time created a little bit of resistance. We don't frame these programs as necessary because he's on the spectrum, we usually frame them as questions, asking him if he wants to try this, or if he could come with us to this visit.

The blood-draw clinic used a similar type of progressive program. They put the tourniquet on the arm first, got him used to feeling that over several visits, and then eventually were able to stick a needle into his arm for vaccines as well. It was awfully hard to get that done, but he's able to tolerate it. We were able to get him to a point where it became more manageable.

The hospital where all of these clinics were offered is a phenomenal facility, and they have outpatient clinics all over our local area to make those resources available.

Not Having the Understanding Was a Struggle

One of the biggest struggles before his diagnosis was not knowing or understanding why things were the way they were: Why does he feel this way or act this way? What are the things that make it difficult for us as a family? One thing that we learned early on after learning more about autism and Asperger's was how to talk to him, set schedules, plan ahead of time, and give reminders in advance. Those things really improved life for us and for him as well. We started seeing fewer meltdowns when we started scheduling things ahead of time, letting him know a week in advance that we are going away for the weekend, and then talking about it leading up to it.

The thing that I struggled with the most as a dad was that I didn't realize how much I had to adapt to what his needs are. Once I got on board with that and started to understand how his mind works a little bit, then I was able to say, "Okay, this is fine. I can work with this." And it didn't take that long. As long as I don't worry so much about the meltdown, but instead try and figure out what caused it, then we'll try and avoid that the next time.

A lot of it for us was trial and error. If it caused a meltdown, we later asked him the reason. When we got a response, then we would try something different. I think now as a thirteen year old, we're a little bit past some of the major meltdowns. We still get some, but we've learned to adapt to try to allow him to be who he needs to be.

Sometimes I struggle with knowing the line between accommodating and setting boundaries. For example, he has his friends online that he plays video games with, and they are a good group of friends. Most of them he actually either goes to school with or has gone to school with, so we know who they are, but there are times that he just doesn't play the same way as they do. He has different goals when he plays, and then when they don't play the same way, he'll end up throwing a fit and throwing the game controller around. I get frustrated that it's going to get broken or that he's going to break something, and so I tell him the consequence that if you break it, you're going to have to buy a new one. I'm not necessarily going to reimburse that. I don't think that method works all the time, but it's something that I'm still trying to figure out. Do I ignore it because he tends to have a shorter meltdown and within an hour he's fine? Some of that adaptation for me is just that's who he is and I just need to accept it.

It's a struggle between wanting to do what society expects of you as a parent versus doing what works for you and your kid. To be honest, I came into fatherhood thinking, I'm going spend a lot of my fatherhood coaching sports. That ended up not being the case at all.

He never really got into sports in any shape or form. Not competitively, anyway. He swims for fun, but not competitively. That was something else that I had to adapt to. My thoughts on what fatherhood is have changed. I don't need to be the father who's going to teach him those kinds of things, and there are other things that he needs to learn from me.

We're starting on working at a job now, just trying to make sure that he understands cutting our grass. You cut the grass. It's a chore, and you get paid for it. Then we'll move on to help him understand other parts of work, but we're starting small.

Although my expectations on fatherhood have changed, I wouldn't say that my life is somehow in a way irrevocably changed in a way that I'll never get back. It wasn't that at all. I recognize that in his accomplishments, whether they be sports related or not, I appreciate so much more than I think I otherwise would have. That came fairly early on after the diagnosis when I started reading about it more. I started understanding a little bit more about how his mind works and what he needs to overcome. Now I appreciate the struggle that he had to go through a lot more.

Acceptance and Looking Forward to the Future

One of the big things is just accepting what is and working with where he's at in the moment. It's only a problem when you start to measure against milestones on an expected timeline, such as getting a job and driving.

There was always an assumption that both of our kids would go to college out of high school. Now I'm starting to think about that. He's only thirteen, but is he going to be ready for it at eighteen the way most kids are? That's unclear to me right now. And what kind of job would he get? It probably wouldn't be something that has a lot of interaction with the general public like in a retail establishment. What are those aspects from a job perspective that may need to be adapted to?

He's already identified that he wants to be a librarian, which is a perfect job for him; he would be happy being surrounded by books all day. At some point we'll have to get him exposed to the specific aspects and expectations of that job. He would love to be able to read all day. I've talked to him about being a proofreader or an editor. He might be good at that.

Ultimately, I would like him to be able to live independently. I want him to be able to get whatever job he wants and be able to live on his own without struggling. That's not something that can be accomplished overnight, but I think that's the biggest goal. If we could get that, I would feel like I did my job to get him ready to function independently, and more importantly, be happy with what he's doing.

All in all, for those who haven't gotten a diagnosis for their child, I strongly recommend that you get an evaluation. I think many parents are afraid to get the official diagnosis because they don't know what it means. Once you have a diagnosis, you have a step toward moving down a different path. It's not a confirmation of how things are going to change for the worse, it's just a different path to get to the same place. There just might be a few more twists and turns. Once the diagnosis is confirmed, it's a way of understanding how the child's brain really functions.

It's about understanding and then acceptance. The purpose of it all is not to change or look for a cure. It's understanding that this is who he is, and then accepting that and really appreciating all of the positives. I think there's sometimes too much attention given to what some people would consider the negatives of being on the spectrum, because there are just as many positives.

We enjoy our son's grasp of language. When he pulls out words that we don't normally use that he reads in a book somewhere, and then uses them in context, it's a fun interaction. I enjoy it at this point, and that's only because I've put some effort into it.

For anyone that's out there that doesn't understand or is afraid, it's really not a negative. I think that's the biggest thing that I want people to understand. I have friends and relatives that don't quite understand what we and what my son goes through in terms of just daily tasks that take more effort than most people are used to, but that's just the way it is. The easiest way to move forward is just to accept that sometimes, those tasks require more effort. And if we accept it, then he won't see it as being any different or feel he needs to be concerned about the fact that he's on the spectrum.

Chapter Five

..•●●•..

Finally, Communication

My name is Mike. I'm an older dad of a son who is now twenty-two and on the spectrum, and he has just graduated from college. We knew something was off very, very early. We did not get an official diagnosis, but we were told that he had developmental disorders from six months old. When we took him to get assistance, the school system at the time provided services for those up to three and said that they could provide us with better services if we leave him without a specific diagnosis. That way, we have the flexibility to give him exactly what he needs. If he was assigned a diagnosis, then we would be limited to the services that fall under that particular rubric.

Therefore, we left him undiagnosed and without an official diagnosis until he was roughly seven. We knew we were going to move from Rhode Island to Louisiana, and with the changes in school systems, we wanted to be sure that we got everything we needed for an IEP before we left. So we took him to a psychologist independent from the school system who gave an official diagnosis which we carried with us to Louisiana. I think playing it that way worked out the best for both him and us. It gave us the most freedom of choice in terms of selecting services and accommodations. Since then he has done extremely well. We were told that if we had done it a little differently, the outcome may have been very different.

On a personal level, when I started to understand that there were some developmental differences, it was an unhappy time for me. I was hoping for a son that I could play ball with, the typical "dad" kind of stuff. I was a fairly active person at the time, and I was looking for a son who would enjoy going to play ball, any kind of ball, or at least hoping that we could ride bikes together. But he wasn't like that. He was more turned in, and he was turned more toward his mom than I might have been happy about. So I was frustrated, and I didn't know how to deal with it. It was hard for me.

There was a turning point, however. I can't remember exactly when it occurred. He was probably in middle school. I read two novels. One of them was The Curious Incident of the Dog in the Nightime, and the other was Marcelo in the Real World. The two of those novels provided insights into the way I was managing my relationship with my son that hadn't occurred to me. For example, there's a scene in The Curious Incident of the Dog in the Nightime where the police are questioning the protagonist who was on the spectrum. He doesn't know how to answer the question because he can't sort out the issue that the question is asking. Was the question about where he was five minutes ago, yesterday, where his head was at the time of the incident, or many other kinds of interpretations of a general question? They asked him another question, in which he also needed to figure out what they actually meant. And it occurred to me that my communication with my son involved an awful lot of questions, because he was not forthcoming with information. In order to figure out what he had done during the day, I had to continually interrogate him, and it was frustrating that he couldn't give the answers.

I realized that he often couldn't answer me because I didn't ask my questions well enough. As soon as I understood that he wasn't not talking to me, but was rather trying to figure out what it was I was actually asking, I could change the way I questioned him. Instead of asking, "What did you do today?" I could ask, "Did you do anything today in particular that you thought was interesting?" That made a difference. All of a sudden, we had communication. It wasn't as free-flowing as I might've liked, but at least the frustration was gone. I could see him pause, which let me know that I asked that question badly, so I'd try again.

He has a number of friends who are also on the spectrum. They might come over and when I would ask them a question, I could see I was doing the same thing to them. I would stop, reconsider the way I was asking, and start again, and then we would have our conversation. Those two books made a huge difference. They provided the original impetus for me to start looking at my behaviors and realizing how I could change rather than mourning the relationship I had lost. Now, that's not to say that I understand my kid, although I think that most parents will say that. However, I'm not as frustrated as I had been, and we have a healthy relationship now.

Finding Common Ground

When he was in eighth or ninth grade, I was still having a hard time looking for things that we could do together. He liked video games. I really don't have much interest in video games. I find them totally unappealing with rare exception, and the games that he particularly likes I find unbelievably tedious. He's not an outdoor person, so we couldn't go outside. And he's not physically robust, so I can't get him to help me with yard work. I was looking for things that we can do together. I remembered that for his birthday in the third grade, we had a bunch of kids over, and we made birdhouses, and we had the best time. There were about six or eight kids and their parents.

I thought that maybe I could get him to come to the shop with me, something that I really enjoy. It's right there, and it's not even physical. Even for just a little while, that would be fun. But I couldn't get him to do it. So instead, we made a party out of it. We invited a bunch of his friends, maybe three or four kids, also on the spectrum, and their dads, and we were out there in the shop making stuff. A makers' club was born, and it's still going on.

After he graduated from high school, I kept it going for the other kids and their dads, and occasionally, a mom or two. We would just make anything we wanted to. It wasn't until my wife came out to the shop after the third or fourth meeting and mentioned to me that we had created something really special. I was able to model behavior for those other dads by having us all work together. We didn't fight anymore. We created a model of communication and cooperation that has changed the way the dads worked with their kids too. The other dads and kids used to fight with each other when we first started. Now, instead of saying, "No, don't do that!" they say, "There's a better way, can I show you?"

It has worked out rather nicely in terms of activities and communication. My son still doesn't like the shop that much, but I can get him to come out and work with me. Every once in a while, he'll bring me something that's broken and ask if we can fix it, and he'll work with me for a while and see if we can't get it fixed. We've finally found something to connect us.

My advice to dads who don't know how to connect with their kid would be to first, listen to Mom. The smartest thing I ever did was not fight my wife. She had a connection with my son already. It was clearly working. I couldn't figure out how to make it work, but when she said do something, even though I hated the idea of doing it, I did it anyway. Whatever it was, I followed her direction. She gave me a lead, and I did it to the best of my ability.

The second thing is to read, do a little research, and pay attention. Even though the two books that I read were novels, whoever wrote them did their homework. They knew what they were talking about, and it was helpful for me.

Around the time of high school graduation, and leading up to it, people were asking, "How is it that you've managed to make a kid on the spectrum successful?" "How do you work with him?" "How do you make it work?"

To them I say, no matter what they do, just love them. When it gets really hard and really frustrating, the only reaction, the only right reaction, is to love them more. And then everything else will come out of that. That's what I'm seeing with the dads that show up at my makers' club. These kids are all really sweet, but they can be really challenging. But you can see that these dads that come to my garage are there because they really love their kids.

There is a lot of pressure from society to have a certain type of child and be a certain type of father, and that not only doesn't work for people on the spectrum, but it causes most of the issues. I have to keep reminding myself, my child cannot be the kid I want him to be. I have to accept the kid that I have and encourage him to be whatever it is that he can grow to be.

Jobs and the Future

One of my sons classmates from college was an intern at my work, and this young man was a brilliant, independent thinker, that had clear goals for himself and a plan for achieving those goals. He would come to me with deep, thoughtful questions regarding the nature of our work. All of the kids I met at the school had some self-motivation. My son, not so much. He wants to do well. He wants to achieve. But thinking ahead is not part of his makeup.

Recently, he came home and told us that he had decided that he couldn't sit around all summer and that he needed to get a job. We were so proud. It's his first job, and we are extremely proud of him for taking initiative, following through, agreeing, cooperating, and doing what needs to be done in order to get a job. We know that eventually, this attitude will grow and mature in him, and he will get the kind of job you expect and hope that your college graduate would move into. There's really no timeline, as long as he's moving forward.

It just so happens that his current job is up the street from where I work, and his hours are close enough to my typical hours that I'm able to drop him off, and my wife would be able to pick him up. Bus service would take him hours to get the three or four miles from that place to our home. Eventually, however, he'll have to learn how to drive. We tried it once when he was in high school. It was challenging for both of us, so we mutually agreed without fighting over it that it wasn't the right time.

I don't know when it's going to happen, but we're both thinking that it might be time to take driving lessons because now there's a need and motivation. And if it doesn't happen, it doesn't happen, but we're both looking forward to the idea that it could happen. It may turn out that he decides that driving isn't really what he wants to do right now. Instead, he could learn to live on his own and move to an apartment that's within walking distance to a grocery store and what have you. It couldn't happen in our town, but eventually, it could happen somewhere close.

There's a fine line between supporting and enabling. We don't want to push him too far in either direction by kicking him out of the house versus letting him live here forever to play video games. We keep him moving forward. For example, we talk about goals far in advance. From the time he was in the first grade, we talked about how he was going to go to college or study something after high school.

We also started telling him that he needed to learn how to cook so he'd be able to feed himself when he's living on his own. We would take him to the grocery store with us and give him half of the shopping list, a cart, and tell him to bring back what he found. Even if he came back with the wrong brand or quantity, we wanted to encourage the success and not the failure. As we kept this up, we started being more specific. Now, if we're in the grocery store and he's unsure of a brand or size, he'll just text us. We could be in a store for thirty minutes, and there would be forty texts between us. Even if what he brings back isn't what we were expecting, we value our relationship more than a brand of spaghetti.

With all we did, we went very slowly, looking forward all the time, moving in the direction that we wanted him to ultimately go. When it comes to the parenting basics, I think for most of us dads, the top of the list is listen to Mom. Be patient. And above all else, when it becomes really hard to love your child, that's the time you need to love them even more. And everything else will come out of that.

Chapter Six

..•●●●•..

Finding My Big "Aha"

Hello, my name is Kevin. I live in Massachusetts and I have a seventeen year-old son that is autistic, and I just love him to death.

He was formally diagnosed at the age of ten or eleven. Prior to that we were thinking it may have been ADHD or OCD. When we got the diagnosis, I didn't really care. We were living real events, real issues, and it was what it was. I don't know that we had any real attachment to it, but it did give us a clearer path forward and I think we were somewhat relieved with that. My wife is a nurse practitioner, and saw early on that there were some learning and behavioral difficulties. She's the one who really started us down the path of finding out what the diagnosis meant and getting him services.

He is adopted, so being adopted from a foreign country and autistic as well, meant that many of his challenges were a combination of him coming to grips with being adopted, as well as him also understanding that he is autistic.

In school, some of the challenges he had were based on his ability to participate as expected in a classroom environment, so he needed a lot of services. The learning part of it wasn't necessarily a problem. He's a very intelligent kid. It was more about how he functions within the rules and expectations of the classroom. I think that was the biggest difficulty that we had.

When he transitioned from elementary school, or 6th grade to middle school, his inability to work within that class environment really became pronounced. At that point we were able to get him into a specialized school. So since about 6th grade he's been at a school for kids with disabilities. At about that same time, when he just started hitting puberty, some of his behavior became a little bit more aggressive and there were some physical issues, particularly with my wife. We had incidents where we needed to call the police to safeguard him and safeguard me. We've had many wrestling matches. There were times where he'd be damaging the house and I needed to stop him. Sometimes I had to hold him down, he even pulled a knife on us once. That actually is what kind of forced the issue to get him into another school.

He struggled at first with the school, and we likened it back to the fact that he never really had closure at his original school. He had a group of kids that he considered his friends. He grew up with them from the first grade. So they understood him to some degree. But some of those kids he's never seen since. So, literally, it was one day he's in the middle school, and because of a specific incident, he could no longer go back. So he never had closure with that school and that kind of drove his attitude toward the new school.

He also has a diagnosis of OCD. So he's a germaphobe and is constantly washing his hands. For some reason, he would think that the new school was filled with germs. That really wrecked havoc with him to the point where he would come home from school and immediately rush right in to take a shower. And that shower might be a four-hour shower. He also wouldn't do certain things, like he would never go in his room because he was afraid he was going to bring the school germs into his room. He still has some germ phobias, but he's built some really strong relationships with his instructors and a group of peers. So it's been good.

For whatever reason, the school that he was going to wants to start moving these kids into more of a "normal" program. So he will actually be transitioning into another school that he helped choose and he's very excited to go. He's excited about it, which is really exciting to us. It's the first time I've ever heard him say, "I'm really excited to go to school." And so that's awesome for us. So we're looking forward to that.

When It Finally Clicked

Over the years our relationship at home has much improved, especially as he's over the puberty hump. He's been through some support with a psychologist, and some other support groups that he's worked with in school. The aggression has stopped, and it is almost nonexistent at this point. It's probably close to a year and a half to two years now since we last had a physical event.

I call myself an old-school father, and I am my father, God bless his soul. I had certain expectations of my son. He was going to be the high school star athlete. I'm a big golfer, so he was going to be a great golfer with me. But those just simply aren't things he's interested in and that's a hard thing to come to grips with.

I would say the big "aha" moment for me was about a year and a half ago where I finally understood that he just thinks differently from me. That was the big "aha" moment. I'm still not a perfect father, and I still rely on my wife to help me. But that was really the big key, determining that he's not wrong, he just thinks differently. So understanding what motivates him, and what drives him, and how he thinks was the big change for me.

I think since then, I've accepted that I'm not going to have a major league baseball player for a son. But I've got a son that's an awesome guitar player, is really intelligent, and I couldn't be prouder of him.

Certainly he's still a teenage kid, and how much does a teenage kid get along with their father anyway? He wants to hang with his buddies. He wants to play his computer games, and things like that, which is fine. But one thing I would say we've kind of connected on is music. We have different tastes in music. But we have come together with going to concerts. We're using those types of events to continue and build our relationship. So that's been positive.

Here's a funny story: I'm a professional, I go to a lot of trade shows and things like that. At these trade shows there are booths and they give you handouts and free stuff to get you to talk to them. This one booth that I was in had this giveaway and it was solving a Rubik's Cube in less than fifteen minutes. It was a little bit different than a normal Rubik's Cube. You could literally unlock it and make it like a long chain. Part of the giveaway was if you could put it back together, and then do the Rubik's Cube in fifteen minutes, they would give you an iPad. That was literally the prize. You could walk away with an iPad.

For four days they had close to a thousand visitors try it. Nobody got the iPad. So I could take the Rubik's Cube and I went home. My son loves Rubik's Cubes and I made the mistake of telling him, "Hey, if you did this at the trade show, you could get an iPad." He didn't have an iPad, so he said "Well, Dad, if I could do it in fifteen minutes, can I get an iPad?" A lot of really smart people had tried this and failed, so I gave it to him and said go for it.

I was going to the bathroom, and, literally, within five minutes, he said, "Dad, I'm done." And I went in there, and sure enough, he had done it. So that's how he got his first iPad. I always tell that story because one part of that "aha" moment I mentioned earlier is that I realized he was smarter than me. And that's kind of a humbling experience for a father. He's smarter than me. He knows it.

What I would say to other dads would be that you've got to be persistent. You've got to find out that "aha" moment, discover what that is. They think differently. They're motivated differently than you, and you need to really understand that. I think the other big thing is, I think they want to have that same close relationship, they just don't know how to express it. So if you enter the situation or the environment with an open mind, and understanding that they really want to have that as well, I think that might be helpful.

Chapter Seven

..•●●•..

Taking Time to Understand

I'm Lucas and my son is Thomas. He is twenty-two and has Asperger's. He was diagnosed in 2002 when he was just about five. It was interesting. We looked into getting a diagnosis because he was just doing things that were a little different than everyone else.

He was first tested when he was five, but I would say the official diagnosis came two years later when he was seven and in first grade because that's when we started noticing the little bits of stimming that he would do. His teacher would tell us that he would walk all the way around at recess, not interact with other kids, and yet he could tell the teacher everything that everyone was doing. My wife was also a schoolteacher, that was her training, so she started recognizing some of the signs before I ever did.

When we were first told the diagnosis and everything, it didn't really hit me because he was still kind of doing everything that a kid would do. He was playing T-ball. He would play soccer. He wasn't the greatest at it, but that was no big deal. He had some friends, and he would play with his animals at home. When it's your first kid, you don't really see those differences.

My wife related to the diagnosis, as she had bouts with anxiety. Even though she never herself got tested, she always kind of related. She would say things like, "That's my kid." "He's like me." So it wasn't a surprise, I guess.

Part of what got me going before I even found Asperger Experts was that I had listened to an audio book called My Strange Son, and it was about a lady from India who taught her son to communicate with her via a machine that they made. Because of the machine her son was able to explain to her what was going on in his mind, that he was having sensory overload. So many things were coming at him so fast that he couldn't process everything. One of the things that she talks about was where he looks up, he sees an airplane, but by the time he recognizes that in his mind, someone is showing him a banana and now the two things don't match. That was frustrating to him; he couldn't absorb the information in time before it disappeared.

Once I understood that, I was able to start to relate more with Thomas, to understand that that's what was going on. Things were coming at him too fast, and when there was too much stimulation, he would shut down. It wasn't until I listened to Asperger Experts that I really realized that he's in Defense Mode and it's like if you had a million people touching you and listening to loud noises at the same time while there were extreme temperature changes and everything going on. So I had to learn about Defense Mode and develop some empathy and understand more about what was going on with my son..

School and Young Adulthood Challenges

Early on, there were no real school challenges. All throughout he never had an IEP or anything. His real challenge was after a while, he got really used to having headphones on. And some teachers didn't like that, but he did it because it was his way of controlling the noise around him.

We would wait a week or two after school started to let the teachers see him without any bias and see him as he is. Then we would sit down and talk with the teachers and explain, "Hey, this is how he is. This is how he reacts, so let him do his thing." With the exception of maybe one or two teachers, they were all very accepting and understanding.

For example: If he had to make a movie for a project, he didn't want other people to see it other than the teacher. He didn't even want to see his own movie. He didn't want other people there. We were always able to make accommodations. So I guess we were just fortunate that our school system had teachers that were very understanding, and he did really well. There were only a couple of teachers that he just didn't get along with, that didn't want him wearing his headphones or things like that.

The big challenge now is driving. He wants to drive, but he can't really go more than maybe fifteen or twenty minutes. It's just too much coming at him. I've never, ever wanted to tell him there's nothing he can't do, but I just don't feel comfortable with him driving. Because the minute he makes the slightest mistake and you have to correct him, he starts to shut down and then it becomes even more unsafe. So he has to rely on public transportation, which where we live is just horrible. Or he'll take an Uber, but even that can become cost prohibitive.

There's a local community college and he went there for two years, now he's going to a major university. I give him a ride in the morning, and then my daughter goes and picks him up at night or in the afternoon. So he gets by with that.

He only has one in-person friend. They've known each other for like five or six years now and they talk almost every day on the phone and over the internet. They have similar interests. He has different groups that he meets with online all the time. So he has a circle of friends, they're just not here. He doesn't go to the mall or do things like that. That's just not him. He'll go online and meet up with his film group, stuff like that.

Moving Forward

He won't get a job, because he can only do school or get a job, one or the other. He's also never gotten a job, so that's going to be interesting for him to have to go out and do that. He worries a lot for me, because I'm his main provider now, and so he gets worried.

The thing that I've got to get him working toward is an independent life. He knows that once he turns twenty-six, he's going to be off of my insurance and he's going to have to get his own. So he knows that the time is coming and that he's going to have to work toward that. But he can't think that far ahead, because then he starts getting anxious. So to make that change I have to slowly get him to start thinking, for example, "Hey, you know, this is what it'll be like if I go away for a week."

He does his own laundry, and he cooks for himself. He cleans up after himself for the most part. So he can do it. It's just that he's scared to go and do it. The rapid change is hard, so if I have to travel for work I let him know in advance that I've got to leave and go out of town. So I can tell him, "Hey, this is what's happening. This is where I'm going to be. This is what is going on." And so he understands those changes. That's kind of how we've been progressing. So I try to anticipate that there could be challenges and try to give him as long a lead time as possible.

In terms of growing up, it's just like dealing with anyone else. If you don't agree on where you're going, where the path is, then you're not going to push him, because the more you push, the more they're going to push back. So I just work slowly with him, without trying to make it a fight. For example, maybe he's not doing his own laundry. So I just say, listen, "If you want clean clothes for school, here's what you're going to need," and I show him how to do the laundry. Every day I'd walk down there and say to him, "This is how you do it, this is how you start it, this is what you've got to do." And then after a while, he learned that he has to do his laundry.

It was a similar situation with cat litter. There was just a way of working with him to get him to see that if he did the cat litter yesterday, he was capable of doing it today too. Now he does it everyday.

I think one thing that's really important for parents to understand, is to know when things are overwhelming. That was a big key for me. Because once I learned that I could see the trigger coming. That was kind of our big breakthrough. Once he realized that I knew he wasn't angry, but just extremely overwhelmed and looking like he was angry, there was a lot more trust. So I try to tell people that. He's not angry, he's just frustrated, and if we let him go a minute, then he'll come back, and it'll be like nothing happened. That has been an incredible way for him and I to communicate. Because he knows that I understand.

So I think that's what I would tell parents. Understand what those triggers are, look for them, try to prevent them if you can. Just let your child know that you understand they're overwhelmed and they're in Defense Mode, and you'll work with them in their own time.

Chapter Eight

..•●●●•..

Finding Connection in the Fight

My name is Jacob, and my son is Josh. Josh is on the spectrum. He was diagnosed in about 4th grade with Asperger's, intermittent explosive disorder, and oppositional defiant disorder.

Josh is a fantastic kid, but when he would become overwhelmed he could become physical. For him it was either fight or flight. And when he would try to flight, someone would stand in a doorway telling him he was not allowed to leave. The caveat is that Josh is not a small individual. At eighteen years old he is six feet, 9 inches and about 280 pounds. At one point, when he was fourteen years old, he was six feet, 4 inches and about 320 pounds. So as you can imagine, when someone is standing in the doorway saying "No, you're not allowed to leave," both people were going through the door.

It has been a challenge, we've been to a children's hospital psych ward eight different times and he's been to six different schools, but I'm happy to report that Josh is now eighteen years old. He is currently off all medications, continuing to do online school, and stands a very good chance of graduating early this year from high school.

My ex-wife and I got divorced when Josh was one. We actually had 50 percent custody until 2013 when I was awarded full custody of all three of my kids. At that particular time I really took a more active role in his treatment plan. I'm a firm believer that it's more of the environment that you allow kids to be in, than necessarily drugging them to get the result you want. I was very against any kind of medication, my fear was that he was just going to sit in a chair and become some kind of zombie. So I was very hesitant to put him on some sort of medication to try to control his behaviors.

His doctor explained to me that as many medications as there are for ADHD, the same number of kinds of pop are out there in America: there's Coca-Cola, there's Pepsi, there's Big K Cola, there's 7 Up, there's Sprite, there's Root Beer, there's Orange Pop, there's Red Pop. Trying to figure out what medicines work for each individual kid is sort of like trying to figure out exactly what kind of pop each kid likes. That gave me a very good understanding that it's not an exact science as you try to identify what works for each kid.

So Josh went through several different medications. One of them caused him to gain weight, another was used to combat weight gain. But at his size and his physicality, I thought it was absolutely necessary to protect others and himself even though I had a rough time accepting the use of the medications at first.

Learning to Adapt

In dealing with his size and physicality I really had to learn how to control my emotions in order to help him control his emotions. I grew up with a father who was a very strong disciplinarian. If you acted up in my dad's house, my dad put it backhand on you or smacked the snot out of you. It was a different environment and a different time. But the main point is, you did not question my dad's rules.

As Josh developed and his behaviors showed themselves more, I learned that I had to deal with things differently. If things escalated, I would put my hands in my pockets and approach him in a nonthreatening manner saying "Hey dude, what do you need? I'm not mad at you. What can I help with?" And that seemed to help bring his level down. In times when he would get physical, I would grab him and put him in a bear hug, and as I was holding him I would calm him down saying, "You're all right." "I'm not mad at you." The pressure of me holding onto him and the tone of my voice seemed to ease him.

That being said, to say that through the years we haven't had a hole or two in our house would be lying. Whether Josh put it there or whether in the emotion trying to grab him, we tussled a little bit, regardless, as I learned to control my emotions, he learned to control his. Through the years, I've got a booming voice. I coached football for years and I learned that me yelling at him did nothing but increase the escalation.

I also had to learn to change my expectations and perceptions. Having autism, it was very difficult for him to look at someone in the eye. That was just something he couldn't do. And when we would go and talk about what his behaviors or what his actions were, he would cover himself with a blanket. While it was different compared to my childhood, I learned that even if Josh wasn't looking at me, he was still listening. The same goes with stimming. I had to learn that it was okay if he fidgeted with something while I was talking to him. Because that gave him a calming sensation, but yet it also allowed him to listen to me. If I tried to force it and physically turn him around and say, "You're going to look at me when I talk to you," all that did was give us another escalation.

In 2015 my older boy joined the Marine Corps and from then on it has just been Josh and I. I think that may have made it a calmer environment for him, and we weren't traveling and going to see his brother play sports all the time. We spent a lot more one-on-one time together.

I watched one of Asperger Experts videos years ago. I believe it was Danny and his dad and it was about how his dad would sit with him and play Pokemon cards. He didn't care for Pokemon, but he learned that by sitting and doing something that his child enjoys, all of a sudden his child would start to open up.

For Josh, his thing was Spongebob. I personally cannot stand SpongeBob. But this one particular Spongebob movie came out and he goes "Dad, I want to watch something, but I don't think you will." And I said, "What, dude?" And then he goes, "Will you watch a SpongeBob Movie with me?" And I said, "You know what? Yes." It was all because I watched that video and it gave me the push to walk through a door that I needed to walk through, and that opened up avenues for me.

I also found out that Josh loves being outside. Sitting in a creek is his zen place. He would rather be sitting in a creek somewhere than doing anything else in the world. So we would go hiking, and on the drive there he would be on his phone watching videos or whatever, and then we would hike and I would even use some of my life experiences to teach him things.

This one particular time, we show up to a trail and it was very crowded. He said, "Dad, I can't." And I told him, "Dude, no problem. Let's check out a different one." So instead of tying to force him to go do something that he wasn't comfortable with, it's about being flexible and the main idea is that we get to do something together.

In going through that, as we were walking on one of the paths, there was a group of maybe ten individuals in front of us. One of them happened to be a sixteen-year-old girl. And Josh being a similar age and a typical kid, was attracted to the girl. I noticed he kept wanting to catch up to them. So we caught up to them several times, and he engaged with them and did that pretty well. On the way home that night he said something about, "Hey, dad, do you ever think I'll have a girlfriend?" I said, "Dude, you are a good-looking kid. You're a big, strong kid. Absolutely."

But here's the kicker: Josh wouldn't brush his teeth. I don't know if it was the sensation of the foaming action, the bristles, or something else. He just wouldn't do it. And at over six feet, I can't hold him down and make him brush his teeth. So I told him in the car that night, "Yes, you're going to have a girlfriend someday. But I guarantee you, no girl is ever going to kiss you if you don't start brushing your teeth. Because that nasty breath is going to be horrible." That boy came home that night and started brushing his teeth.

So I was able to use life experiences to sort of adapt some of his behavior. But it couldn't be what I wanted for him. It had to be what he wanted. I think our biggest thing is we built trust. He learned that he could trust me above everybody else. I was a safe spot. I held him accountable. If he got physical, I made him write an apology letter. If he hurt someone or damaged property, there would be a disciplinary action. But I didn't hold that against him after he paid the price. No matter what he did, my love for him was unconditional. I was not going to change.

Advice for Other Dads

My biggest advice would be not to take tense moments personally. When your child is yelling f- bombs at you, saying things like "stay the blank away from me," or "I hate you," those are not easy things for a parent to hear. But if you realize that it's not personal, and that in their minds they are overwhelmed and don't know how else to react or what else to do, that can be very helpful in those moments.

For Josh, it's like walking him off a windowsill. When he's in that escalation mode it's not the time for a teaching moment. You cannot try to teach someone when they are overwhelmed. Once it is later and they have calmed down, that's when you do the after-action review and say, "Hey dude, you wanted a candy bar. But yet you ran over, grabbed the candy bar, screamed, 'I'm going to take this! I'm going to take this!' That didn't get you what you wanted. How could you have gotten what you wanted? Your way of doing it didn't work, so let's try it this way the next time." We worked on these types of things over and over again, but because we were willing to work through those scenarios, it helped him and he now knows how to ask for things.

I've also had to learn that it's sort of give-and-take as well. I'll be honest, I have a very high standard in my house. I will not live in clutter. I can't stand it. I'm a bit OCD, but cleanliness is just not on the list of Josh's priorities. I do laundry and as soon as it comes out of the dryer I fold my shirts a certain way. I spent eight years in the military. Josh, on the other hand, would rather have his clothes all over the floor of his room.

As he got older, I would say things like "Dude, it's your responsibility to get your clothes up to order. Don't come crying to me if you're out of underwear and you haven't brought it up to the laundry. You're old enough. You're responsible enough." I called up a friend of mine whose son was also on the spectrum, and it turns out she was struggling with the exact same thing. Sometimes you just have to concede certain things.

Josh is in his own unique world. He sees things differently than I do. And that's what makes this world so wonderful: You and I are not the same. We're different. And that's a wonderful thing. You don't have to do things exactly the way I do. I just ask that they get done.

Chapter Nine

..••●•..

Helping Him Find His Path

My name is Hank. My son Hendrick was kind of slow to develop and had some problems with speech development. He didn't really talk very much until he was over two years old. He was slow to be potty trained.

When he was about three, we started taking him to different doctors, trying to get a diagnosis of what was going on. There was talk of learning disabilities, but nobody really could pin down exactly what it was. At that same time he was getting into trouble at school, and we had to leave and go to another daycare.

At some point, when he was around three and a half or four, we started taking him to speech therapy and things picked up at that point. He seemed to pick up more of an interest in talking and learning about language and things like that, but school and day care was still a struggle. He wouldn't do anything that anyone told him to do. He was very obstinate. He wouldn't pay attention. He would only do what he wanted to do. When they were trying to do things like group activities, he would interrupt to try to get everybody's attention.

We put him in a Montessori environment after moving and he did a little bit better there. But ultimately, we were still seeing a neurologist/psychologist and still weren't getting any sort of definitive diagnosis of what was going on. There was some talk of learning disabilities and communication disabilities and even some discussion of possible autism, but nothing concrete.

Again we moved for a job and put our son in a private school and very quickly found that it didn't work out due to discipline problems. After that we decided that maybe public schools were the way to go. One of the teachers there had a daughter with Asperger's syndrome, and it was at that point when Hendrick was maybe six or seven that he was finally unofficially diagnosed.

I'm a librarian, and my wife works with books, so we're both big readers and we started reading up on everything we could about Asperger's syndrome. We both learned and thought "Hey, this does sound a lot like what's going on with him." There were other things going on, too, but I think the Asperger's part was a pretty big chunk of it. Later on, he was diagnosed with ADHD.

However, the diagnosis was not the solution to all of our difficulties. He wouldn't study, and he still wouldn't listen unless it was something that he was really interested in. He would still be disruptive to the rest of the class. That's been his career pretty much all the way through high school. We tried to lure him with promises of Pokemon cards or video games and he wouldn't change his ways for that. We also tried threatening to take away video games or threatened to take away other things, and that wouldn't do anything either. No matter what we tried, there was really no way to motivate him.

The teachers felt the same way. At times, they would just take him out of the environment as opposed to trying to get him to fit in. He'd go work in the library. You can't do a whole lot for him when he's at school. My wife and I both work, so there's not really any way we could hold his hand all day long. It was never really something that was possible. But we did have some very patient teachers and some very patient administrators, and I feel like that's the main reason he made it through to graduation.

After High School

After high school, his mom really wanted him to go to college, as did I. I think he could be successful if he found the right degree or the right program, but he has never found something that interests him enough to do it. He started going to the local community college here and he just would not do the work. He would skip class and wouldn't do any of the basic things to succeed, at all. So it was a waste of our money and a waste of our time to send him.

He was content to stay at home and play video games, but we pushed him to get a job. He's had several jobs since he was eighteen, maybe six or seven, mainly retail. He worked at the Goodwill going through their donations of boxes. He also worked at Walgreens and at a department store nearby. He was also a stock boy. So he's worked at several different places. Right now, he works at GameStop part-time. He also has a job at Best Buy. He's had a lot of the same issues with his jobs that he did at school. If he wasn't interested in it, he wasn't motivated to do it. That's just kind of been his frame of mind from day one.

He's now twenty-five and he lives at home. His mom still washes his clothes and generally cooks for him. He does know how to do these things, but his mom's a bit of a spoiler, so she tends to do just about everything for him. I don't know if it would change anything if he had to do his own clothes, but he doesn't seem very motivated to move out. That being said, I love having him around. He's a great kid. We really have fun together now that he's a grown up. But it's just been a struggle to get him to take his life seriously, and think about what he wants to be, and work towards that goal.

Advice for Other Dads

I would say to other dads that you have got to be patient. You can't try to rule them. You can't try to be forceful with them verbally. Be aware of your approach to the child. You've just got to find out what's the best thing for your child, try to find their bright spots, and identify what's important to them.

Maybe encourage them to take classes or go into a career that appeals to them as opposed to something that maybe you feel like they should do. Don't try to fit them as a square peg into a round hole. Be aware of what they're good at, what their strengths are, and what their weaknesses are. Then try not to fight them.

I really kind of watch out for those kinds of people in the media, like Sheldon on Big Bang, and other people that are on TV now. I'm very proud to have Hendrick as my son. I'm proud to have an Asperger's kid. He's still got so much potential if he can figure out his way. So I'm hopeful and I know that it's hard, but if you're patient and you stick with it, I think you can have some really great things happen.

Chapter Ten

..•●●●•..

A Special Bond with My Daughter

My name is Owen. I am fifty-six years old and a father of five daughters. My fourth oldest child is the one that has been diagnosed as on the spectrum. It was a very interesting journey as we tried to find out what was happening with her and getting the help and resources that she needed. At the end, we actually ended up discovering that I also had it!

I always had an idea that something was different about me in the way I related to other people, and the way I interacted with my peers. There was always something off, and my peers knew it but did not know how to explain it. I knew it too, but didn't know how to explain it either. I came from a generation where we didn't believe in doctors. We did not believe in going to seek medical help unless it was absolutely vital. So going and getting diagnosed at a young age was something that never would have happened.

As a child I was labeled and called every kind of thing. I was "hardheaded," I was "rebellious," I was "different," I was "weird," I didn't want to "conform." I did all the little nonsocial things, but I was told that I was "too smart" and "too verbal," so nothing ever really came of it. I went through my life just saying, "Ok, I'm just really different. I'm going to avoid people and try not to deal with them as much as possible." I became a hermit in the sense that I just went to work, came home, minded my business, and didn't bother with anybody. As a result, it began to affect my work life. It began to affect my family life. I had all kinds of struggles. I couldn't relate to other people, other people couldn't understand me. Looking back, it is extremely clear-cut that I've had Asperger's all my life, but it just wasn't obvious until my fourth child.

Father and Daughter versus the World

Some of the similarities we picked up right from the start. The way she interacted with people, the way she would hide from people, the way she would talk to people. Sometimes she would be so soft you couldn't hear her, and then sometimes so loud you could hear her a mile away. Very smart, very intelligent, but very people-averse. She did not want to be around people or talk to them. It reminded me of when I was young, I would go and hide in a tree house that I made. Other times I would run into the woods with my sleeping bag and bury myself under leaves and hide. Likewise, she built a little hidey place under her bed where she would run to when she was stressed out.

We were just so similar, it wasn't long before people started saying to her the same things that they said to me. "What's wrong with you?" "Why can't you just fit in?" And so that began to be the first inkling that there might be something different worth checking out. So we got her evaluated and they came back with the diagnosis of Asperger's. That's when the light went off for me.

So upon talking with my wife, I went to get checked out as well and was subsequently diagnosed with Asperger's. When I heard those words, it was like a great burden had been lifted. I'll never forget that moment when I finally got that diagnosis. I literally sat in a parking lot and cried for about an hour because it all made sense. Everything that I had dealt with, all the misunderstanding, all of the "he's weird" and "he's different" finally made sense. I was now welcome on earth. I now have a place. I don't fit in, but I was never made to fit in. I was already made different from the jump. Others just did not recognize what I was dealing with or how I was wired and how to interact with me. As a result I was made to feel bad, but the reality was on them because they did not know.

Because of our mutual diagnosis, my daughter and I have ended up having an extraordinarily special bond. She knows where I am coming from, and I know where she is coming from. I know her feelings. I know her emotions. One of the things that we say all the time between us is "Asperger's is what's right with me." We never say that it's what's wrong with us. It's always what's right with me. It's who we are, and we embrace it. She embraces it and I embrace it. We allow ourselves to be fully different regardless of what other people think.

To be able to be on the same level with one another has been such a blessing. It's been so amazing to see this child that has been so shy, quiet, and reserved finally start coming out of her shell. She ended up joining band and even doing cheerleading for a short season. She didn't like it, but she tried it and began to do things that were more people oriented.

Because she felt she was understood at home, she had the information and tools to understand that it was okay when she felt like she was different. She had a place to go where she could be herself as opposed to feeling different, weird, and pushed off to the side. The validation and knowing there's somebody there that says," I know where you are because I've been where you are." Or "I still am where you are and have moments with withdrawal and breakdowns," is really just a game-changer.

Other than developing that mutual understanding of one another, there are a lot of things in my life that I have learned that I have been able to pass onto her. One of the things that I've done over the years is that I allow myself the time each day to make a "what I've done" list as opposed to "what to do" list. A lot of people start the day and say, "I need to do A-B-C-D-E-F-G." Opposite of that, I go and say, "I have done A-B-C-D-E-F-G." Doing that helps both of us not get so overwhelmed with a lot of the tasks that come our way.

Another thing that I've tried to teach her is that it's okay to have stressful moments and times. It's okay to feel what you are feeling, take a break, and walk away from situations. She's an artist and a musician, she loves to draw and do things like that. Creativity is her thing. So even now that she is in college, she knows that it's perfectly okay to go draw and block stuff out in her hidey hole. So that has been very helpful in regard to processing and dealing with things even though she is away at college in a dorm. No matter where she is when she gets stressed out and overwhelmed, she's able to deal with it.

I think the last major thing I taught her, is that not everybody is going to understand. Especially people who aren't on the spectrum or aren't directly connected to somebody that is. Those people are not always going to understand how to respond or how to speak, and that's going to be hard to understand. It's important to not always be defensive, nor let conversations like that let you meltdown. Sometimes you have to leave those conversations, and then maybe come back to them when you are ready to deal with them. In addition to that, it is always okay to filter things out that you don't need to be involved in. It's okay to say no. She's a very people-person in the sense that she wants people to like her, so teaching her how to say no has been another big thing.

Advice for Other Dads

Love your child, no matter how different your expectations of what you think they should be or could become are. We have to learn to embrace the differences. When we learn to embrace the differences, it's a much better journey for all of us. There are a lot of parents—and dads in particular that want to live vicariously through our children to the point that we want to force them to do the things that we failed in doing. (Becoming a professional athlete, or whatever) You cannot do vicarious living through them. You have to let them chart and create their own path as opposed to forcing them down the path that you want them to go.

You've got to love them despite their differences. You've got to learn from them; there is so much to learn. Take the time to listen to them. What they're saying may be seen as different to you, but it's not necessarily wrong. It's just different, and different is not a bad thing. Just because somebody is different doesn't mean they're not awesome. Everybody in the world has their individual challenges. Whether it's asperger's, autism, whatever we're dealing with, we have our own individual challenges. We have got to learn to love and see each other despite the differences that are immediately presented to us.

I am blessed to be a coach of athletes, and I've been coaching for years. I have all different types of athletes in my program. One of the things I try to create is a culture of success through embracing differences. I tell them, "Don't let anybody else find your success for you. You can define your own path to success."

So with the kids on my teams, with my daughter, with you who is reading this, let them define themselves. Give them the tools that they need, yes, encourage them, but you can't define it for them. You've got to let them find their way, and if it's different, it's different. Whatever it is, let it be that. Embrace it and encourage them in it. They will thank you for it. Your relationship will blossom because of it. They will be a better person because you have not forced them to fit into a hole that was not made for them.

A Final Note

Thank you so much for reading this book, supporting our work and helping us get this message out to more parents of kids on the spectrum. If you like what you've read, we invite you to join us at www.AspergerExperts.com for online discussions, helpful videos and articles, as well as more books, courses and helpful materials in your Asperger's journey.

We're a small team of passionate people with Asperger's and Autism trying to make a difference in the world, and do this full time, so again, thank you. Asperger Experts was founded on the belief that it is possible for people with Asperger's and Autism to live complete, fulfilling lives and the stories in this book are proof that with the right focus and determination, that belief can become a reality.

Remember: People do the best they can with the emotional capacity they have.

— The AE Team

www.AspergerExperts.com